Copy, Play & Learn

Guitar

the EASY, FUN WAY
for young people

BY BRYCE LEADER

Copyright ©2011-2012 Bryce Leader
First Edition 2013
ISBN (book) 978-0-9874822-0-4
ISBN (recording) 978-0-9874822-1-1

Author: Leader, Bryce.

The author wishes to thank the following people for their assistance in producing this book and CD recording: The Honourable Justice David Ashton-Lewis, Sue Roberts, Naomi Leader, Brendan Morris, Noelle McAlister, Tim Brown, Andrew Hobbler, Scott Mason, Ross Leader, Chris Jordan, Nigel Baker, Susana Bosanac, Adrian Stuckey and Carol Chambers.

To purchase copies of this book, please contact Bryce Leader on:
EMAIL: info@copyplayandlearn.com.au
WEBSITE: www.copyplayandlearn.com.au

Prepress artwork by: Carol Chambers - art@firstprint.com.au

Contents

Guitar lessons for children.
The Goals, challenges, insights and solutions.

THE GOALS

As music teachers, our goal is to encourage a long term love of learning and set the students under our tutelage on the best possible path toward helping them reach their potential. Often, short term goals are to teach students to play fluently and process and interpret the signs and symbols that make up written music.

The children we teach have a single goal - they just want to be able to play the guitar. However, associated with this single, simple goal is a host of expectations. Young children expect to learn quickly, they want their lessons to be fun and easy, they want to learn with minimal practice and they want to be able to play the kind of music they hear through the media.

THE CHALLENGES

Many guitar teachers have no doubt turned away potential students because they are seen as being too young. Most guitar teachers will consider teaching a student only when they are about nine years of age or older. Poor fine motor skills, a limited concentration span and the inability to understand the complex musical components of written music are reasons often cited for starting lessons later. Those teachers who do accept students at an early age often find that the frustration that occurs in lessons and at home in practice time brings about a negative experience.

Reading the music contained in most beginner books is difficult. Reading music requires analysis, thought and concentration. A child is required to process the pitch and duration of many notes many times within a short, 'simple' piece, as well as making sure that their posture and hand positions are correct. How often have you, as a guitar teacher, been struggling to teach your child something like, 'Mary had a little Lamb?' This is a song that contains notes of only four different pitches and three different rhythmic figures. It shouldn't be hard to learn, but it is.

THE INSIGHTS

Consider that same child who, unable to play 'Mary had a Little Lamb,' then effortlessly presents you with the opening riff to 'Smoke on the Water' at their next lesson. Astonished, you ask, "How did you learn to play that?" "Oh, my Dad showed me," is often the reply. The young student has just showed you the method of learning to play the guitar that is most effective for them, and that is by imitation. Whether they are learning to speak, write or perform a sporting activity, a young child learns best and naturally by imitating the actions of those around them.

To the young child, a positive and pleasurable dining experience, it could be argued, makes them conscious of the restaurant, McDonalds. For the child who cannot yet read, through repetitive exposure to the McDonalds symbol, even though they may not yet be able to "sound out" the word, the child knows that the writing underneath the Golden Arches says McDonalds. When learning to read words, the association of that word to a picture or symbol is an important first step.

THE SOLUTIONS

"For children to learn effectively, they must see their lessons as being relevant, interesting and pleasurable…" This is a statement that most school teachers and educators would recognise and is just as relevant to guitar teachers. This book, 'Copy, Play and Learn Guitar…' allows teachers and students to achieve their goals and realise their expectations by making use of the natural and preferred ways children learn, and that is by imitation, repetition and association, while being relevant, interesting and pleasurable.

By observing and imitating a visually logical pattern of notes as demonstrated by their teacher, a young student can confidently play the easy and fun songs and pieces in this book to a vibrant backing track. The child develops the ability to read music at their own pace, as they play. The burden of the young musician having to process pitch and rhythm simultaneously many times very quickly and independently is eased. Their focus can then extend to other tasks such as finger placement and aural awareness, and the student has time to gather their thoughts before attempting the next phrase.

What appears easy to adults can be quite challenging for the young beginner guitarist. The simple act of plucking a string with the thumb in time with music can be difficult and then changing to another string is even more so. This book is designed so that in the initial stages, one fine motor movement at a time is isolated and repeated in the context of a song. As the student progresses, patterned finger dexterity movements of the fretting hand and actions of the thumb are combined. The pattern may be repeated on a different string or different string combination. The songs may often be long, but generally only have two or three themes for the student to become familiar with.

Complex musical terminology has been minimised. This book contains no key or time signatures and even though notes are written as crotchets, quavers and minims, no attempt has been made to tell the student of their duration. The student will identify visually and aurally that some notes last longer than others, but the exact note length in terms of the number of beats is a subject for subsequent books the student will use as they progress.

The rhythm of the melody of a song or piece the child is about to play is easily learned through singing and clapping the rhythm of the words with which it is associated. For example the words "Tid-y up your bed-room," or, "All night I lay dream-ing," are associated with the rhythm, "te,te,te,te ta,ta". Such rhythms recur in songs throughout the book. The student is able to relate a rhythm to a previously learned piece, and is readily able to identify and play it.

In a similar way, the young guitarist associates the words, "I love football," with the notes C,G,F,C. This is one of several identifiable recurring melodic fragments that appear in a number of songs in differing harmonic settings throughout the book.

To ensure that this guitar teaching method is relevant, interesting and pleasurable, students are provided with contemporary, humorous and exciting songs, all of which have backing tracks that give the student an immediate sense of beat and rhythm. This book turns monotonous preparatory exercises into real songs. The melody that the students play may be simple, but the harmony twists and weaves to the backing of a real band with singers and electric guitars. This makes playing finger exercises much more vibrant and enjoyable and, therefore, much more likely to be practised. Children feel like they are playing along with a professional rock band. The stories draw themes from the day to day experiences of children and are based around the central character, Simon, his friends, family and their social interactions. Interests such as bike riding, surfing and skateboarding feature and provide material for the lyrics, as do sleepovers, smelly socks and dog farts. A story sprinkled with humour develops with each song and students can enjoy linking them together. There is also a level of humour that may engage parents and give them a bit of a giggle as they help their child practise.

Children are often confused by the pitch of notes. They often think that notes are placed randomly on the stave and don't perceive the connection between the alphabetical order, the ascending pitch of notes and the likely position on the guitar fingerboard. In the 'Copy, Play and Learn Guitar' method, there are exercises the student can do, and flash cards that the teacher can make use of, to ensure that the student knows the names of the notes or can at least work them out. Many of the pieces in this method are designed to facilitate easy note recognition, the relationship to pitch and subsequent position on the guitar finger board.

In becoming an independent note reader, there are sometimes sections within the songs in this method, and indeed whole songs themselves, which encourage the student to play without first hearing or seeing what their teacher does. These are the first steps toward mentally processing pitch and rhythm. In these cases, there are whole bars that may contain notes of just one pitch thus allowing students plenty of time to process.

HOW TO TEACH THESE PIECES

To ensure the success in playing each piece, follow these few basic steps:

- Break down the learning process into small, manageable parts and focus on one task at a time.

- Draw attention to the rhythms in the piece and clap them saying "ta" for crotchets and "te te" for quavers. Ask the student to repeat the rhythms in the spaces provided in the score and audio.

- Draw attention to the pitch of the notes, say the note names in time with the rhythm and then ask the student to copy you.

- Show the student where the notes required to play the piece are on the guitar. Place a sticky white dot or self-adhesive label (available from newsagents) on the fret board indicating where to place the fretting finger.

- A pattern often exists in the pieces making learning them easier. Draw the student's attention to it or see if they can discover it for themselves.

- Play the tune and ask the student to copy you in the areas marked ✗. ✗✗. ✗✗✗.

- Play the tune in time with the recording.

Teaching points in the book are directed to the student but aimed at the teacher and are espoused by the likeable, Rockin' Judge and other characters in the book. For more detail on the aims and teaching points of each piece, please visit the website, **www.copyplayandlearn.com.au** and click the *resources* section before selecting, *a guide for teachers*.

RECOMMENDATIONS AND SUPPLEMENTARY ACTIVITIES

- In learning these pieces and songs it is very important that they be played with the accompanying recording. This helps establish the young musician's sense of beat and rhythm.

- Children can tire quickly and often a change in activity may be needed. A good exercise is to draw the student's attention to the fact that music is written on a stave made up of lines and spaces. Ask your student to remember that the notes in the spaces spell FACE and the first letter of the words in the saying, Every Good Boy Deserves Fruit is a way of remembering the names of the notes on the lines. (Refer to p.19.) It is recommended that the note name not be written above the note on the stave.

- Make use of the flashcards provided at the back of the book to help reinforce the material learnt.

- Many pieces in the book make use of a step-wise ascending pattern. The names of the notes in the pattern are thereby presented in alphabetical order. The song, 'I Love Football' (p.24), is the first piece to use a descending step-wise pattern of notes, the names of which will be presented in alphabetical order but backwards. A fun activity is to drill the letter names alphabetically from A to G and then backwards, from G to A.

- Teachers could draw attention to the contour of the melody and ask the student if they would expect it to sound high or low as the music moves up and down.

- Sometimes notes move by a leap rather than a step. Teachers can help students work out the note names by counting up the lines and spaces. (See p.21)

- Despite having drilled the note names and the note's location on the guitar, teachers should not be too concerned that the young student won't read the notes straight away and continues to look at the teacher's fingers and to the teacher for direction. Teachers should persist with note reading tasks; however, children will learn to read as they work their way through the book.

- As the student progresses through the book, they may start to show signs of becoming independent. There are several songs in this book where such students can showcase these abilities.

- Sticky dots placed on the guitar fret board can serve to indicate the location of the notes on the guitar fingerboard, and students at this early stage should pluck the string with their thumb rather than a pick.

- For teachers, the objectives and teaching points associated with each piece may be found on the website **www.copyplayandlearn.com.au** by clicking the *resources* section before selecting, *a guide for teachers*.

WORK THAT THUMB!

Teacher　　　　　　　　student

Rockin' Judge says...

This piece focuses on moving the thumb from the first to the second strings in time with the music.

- E sounds higher than B. That is why it is written higher on the stave.
- The repeat sign tells the musician to go back to the beginning and play the piece again.
- The simile mark tells you to play the music written in the bar before. In this case, the teacher plays what's written and the student copies in the "simile" bar.

E. Open 1st string

B. Open 2nd string

An "open" string is a string plucked without it being held down on a fret.

8

The first three open strings

Rockin' Judge says...

Let's get that thumb working a little harder and move it between the first, second and third strings

This Is the note, G, and is the open 3rd string. It is written lower on the stave than the other notes so it will sound lower. (It will have a lower pitch)

These notes are called **Ta** and these notes are **te te** Make sure you clap the rhythm and name the notes in time with the recording. **Te te** notes are faster than **Ta.** Look at the piece, "Work that Thumb". Can you find the same notes and rhythms written in this song?

Sometimes students will forget the note names. Take a little time out and revise using these prompts.

Lines

Spaces

Every Good Boy Deserves Fruit

F A C E

HOMEWORK

tacet

Tid – y up your bed – room,   put a – way your school clothes,

Make use of the straw broom,   do not have a run – ny nose.

Wash your dish – es in the sink,   use de – od – or – ant, you stink,

Eat your din – ner, chew your food,   most of all, I hate to do,

home – work,   home – work,   home – work,   home – work,

home-work,   home – work,   home – work,   home – work.

Rockin' Judge says…

- Hi there Groovers. You might notice some rhythms and notes that we've used before, except now we have words attached to them. We can play our first real song!
- Can you tell your teacher which notes are **ta** and which are **te te**? What are the note names and where do you find those notes on the guitar?
- Ask your teacher to clap the rhythm and sing the words and you copy them in the repeat bar.
- Watch your teacher and copy what they play. They may need to say the note names for you as they play.
- **Tacet** means "don't play" and the "8" is really there just for your teacher. There's some electric guitar being played at this time.
- The repeat sign facing the other way ‖: says to repeat from here.

10

Homework

At the beach.

AT THE BEACH

All night I lay dream-ing, waves break on the shore-line,

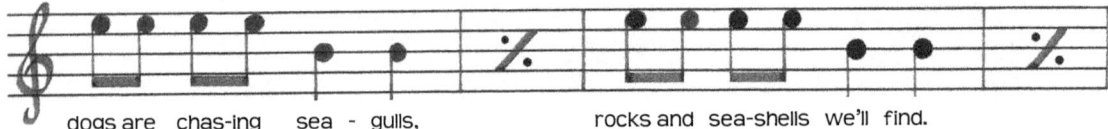

dogs are chas-ing sea - gulls, rocks and sea-shells we'll find.

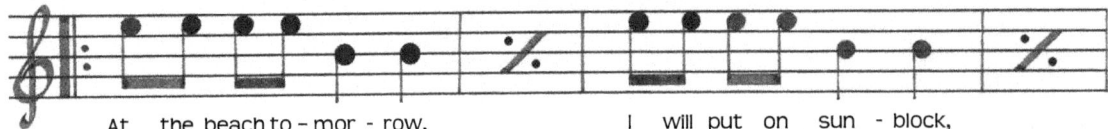

At the beach to-mor-row, I will put on sun - block,

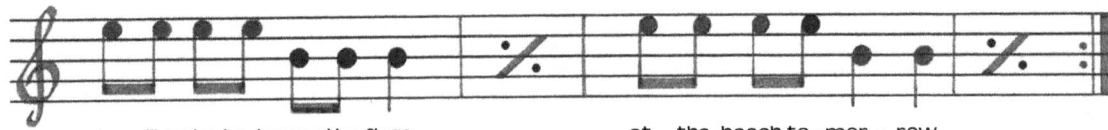

x3

I will swim be-tween the flags, at the beach to-mor-row.

Rockin' Judge says...

- Remember to say the words, clap the rhythm and name the notes.
- Can you recognise the rhythm of the words, "all night I lay dream-ing" or "at the beach to-mor-row"?
- Can you find that same rhythm in "Homework"?
- Can you clap that rhythm for your teacher?
- What are the names of the notes?
- Which notes sound higher and which sound lower?
- Which string sounds high and which sounds lower?

FOUR STRING ROCK

tacet

Rockin' Judge says...

This is a D note. It is the open 4th string. Look at how low on the stave it is. Would it sound higher or lower than the notes we've learnt?

- Can you show your teacher which are the high sounding strings and which are the low sounding strings on your guitar?
- Notice that every two lines are the same except the rhythm changes. Can you tell your teacher what the rhythms are?

MY SOCKS SMELL

My   socks   smell,   my   socks   smell,

your   socks   smell,   your   socks   smell,

Yes, my socks they smell,   yes, my socks, they smell.

Rockin' Judge says...

Hi Groovers! It seems like you're coming along very nicely. I think it's time that we started to use the fingers on our fretting hand.

- Ask your teacher to place a sticky dot on the first fret of the first string and mark it "**F**".

This is what "**F**" looks like on the stave. It's placed just above E on the stave. Will it sound higher or lower than E? Have a listen!

- Make sure you press down on the F note firmly with your first finger as you pluck the 1st string.
- Sing the song and clap the rhythm of the song after your teacher.
- Name the notes and clap the rhythms

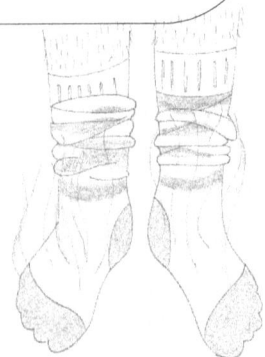

14

Our friend, the Judge.

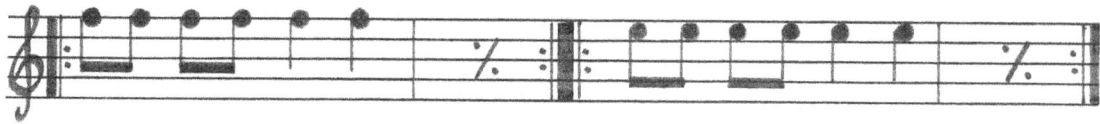

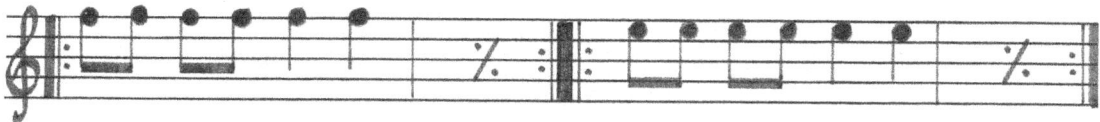

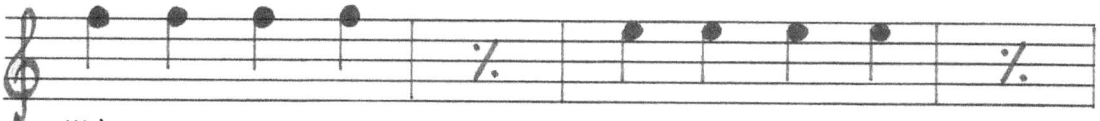

We've a good friend, he's a rock star.

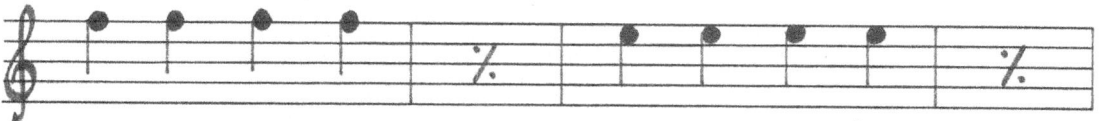

We call him "Judge," we play gui - tar.

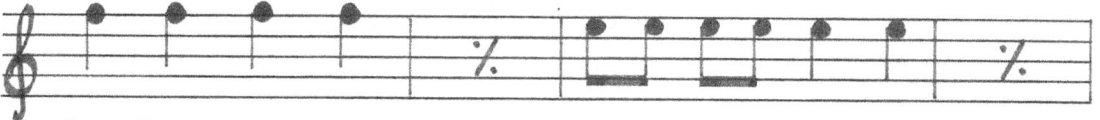

He likes to play, 'lec - tric and ac - ou - stic.

He knows so much, helps us with our mus - ic.

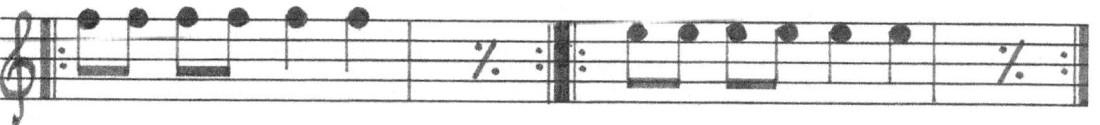

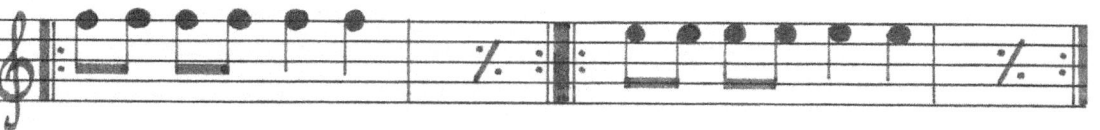

Hi, I'm Dorothy, Simon's sister. My brother and I are big fans of the Judge. You might be able to find us in the front row at his latest concert. There seemed to be a few famous faces there too! Can you find them?

The judge was too bashful to talk about a song we wrote about him so he said to pass this on.

- This is a song based on a finger exercise where you need to coordinate your left and right hands. You have to press down on the F note quite hard as you pluck the 1st string with your thumb.
- When you take your finger off the F to play E, don't lift it very far. Keep it in position so it's ready to place on the F note again.
- Don't forget! Sing the song, clap the rhythms and name the notes.

I like cake and custard

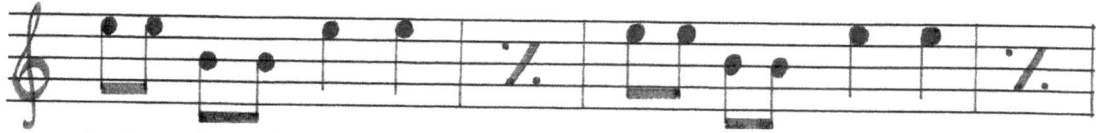

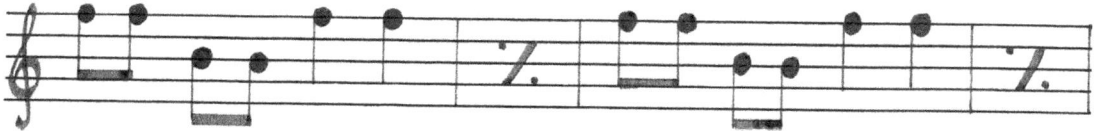

I like cake and cus - tard,   I like cake and cus - tard.

You like cake and cus - tard,   you like cake and cus - tard.

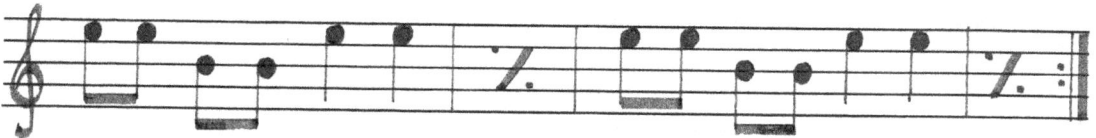

We like cake and cus - tard,   we like cake and cus - tard.

Thanks, Dorothy for your kind words. This song is about one of Simon's favourite desserts, cake and custard.

This song will challenge your coordination skills! You'll have to move your thumb from the 1st to the 2nd strings and back again as well as move your fretting finger on and off the first string. Good luck!

- Remember to clap the rhythm as you sing the song after your teacher in the "repeat" bars.
- You should be getting to know this rhythm fairly well by now. What is it? What other songs use it?

SCHOOL TODAY

I   have   trav - elled   a   long   way,

Just   to   come   to   school   to - day.

Three   o' - clock   I   say   "hip,   hoor – ay!"

Then I   do it   all a - gain a – noth – er   day.

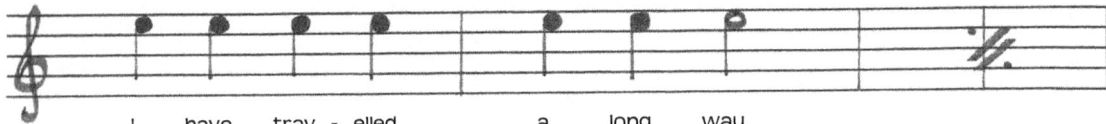

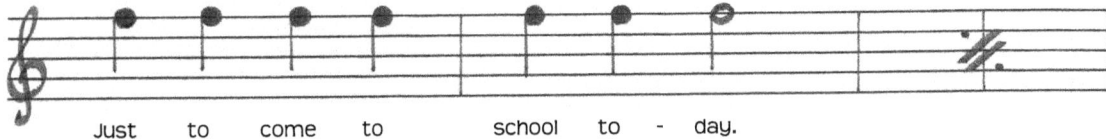

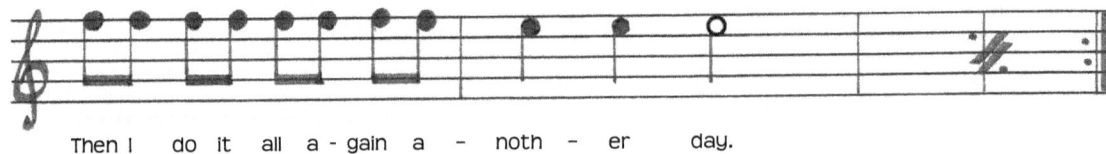

Rockin' judge says...

It's time to learn a new note!

This note is called "**G**". Ask your teacher to put a sticky dot on the 3rd fret of the 1st string. Hold this note down firmly with your third finger as you pluck the 1st string.

- Some of you Groovers might get confused as to which "G" you are supposed to play because now you know two of them! Just remember, it is written high upon the stave so it will sound high. You remember where the high notes are?

- Your teacher will tell you that the   sign means to repeat.

- Try to learn the names of the notes from memory.

- Show your teacher where the notes go up and down.

- What is the name of the note that you start on? What are the next notes? And the notes after those?

- Do you notice that when the notes go up, they go up in alphabetical order?

- What happens to the alphabetical order when the notes go down?

Steps and Leaps

What's the difference between a step and a leap?

I think that you may already know the answer to this question. Let me explain. If you were to walk up a flight of stairs, one step at a time, and one foot after the other, it could be said that you are moving, "up by step". If you managed to jump from the bottom step to the top step, it could be said that you are moving up by a leap. You could also go *down* the stairs by a step or by a leap.

Up by step   **up by a leap**   **down by step**   **down by a leap**

Music, written on the page is said to resemble stairs. Sometimes music moves up or down by a step, or up or down by a leap. Remember the prompts to recall names of the notes on the lines and spaces?

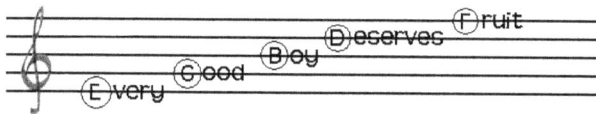
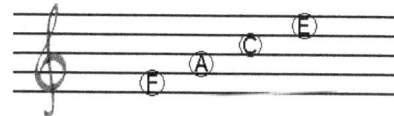

These notes on our "musical flight of stairs" (known as the staff or stave) are going up, not by a step but by a leap. Below are the same notes, but written out by step. Can you write the note names below each note?

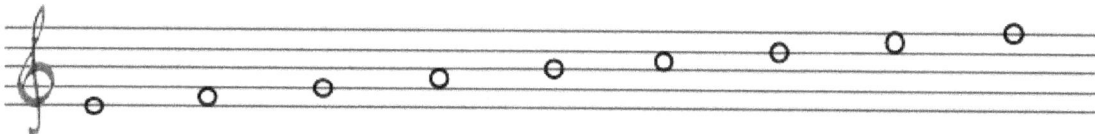

— — — — — — — —

What can you tell about the order of the notes as they move up by step? They are in **alpha _ _ _ ical** order. We already know a high, **"G"** note. Although it's not included in our prompts, let's include it on our staff anyway.

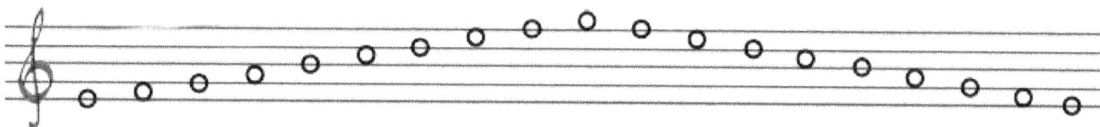

— — — — — — — — — — — — — —

- Can you re write the note names, but this time, include the names of the notes as they go down?
- What do you notice about the order of the note names when the notes go down? The alphabetical order goes

b _ _ k w _ _ ds.

- Just remember, that in our *musical* alphabet, we only go up to the letter **"G"**. After G we start again at A.

SOGGY SANDWICHES

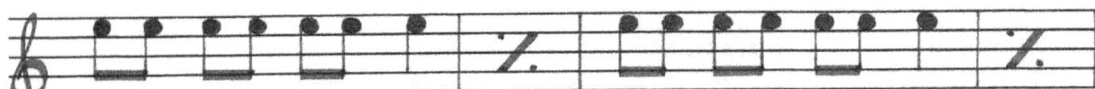

I hate sog-gy sand-wich-es,   I hate sog-gy sand-wich-es

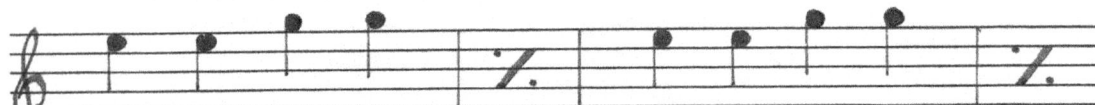

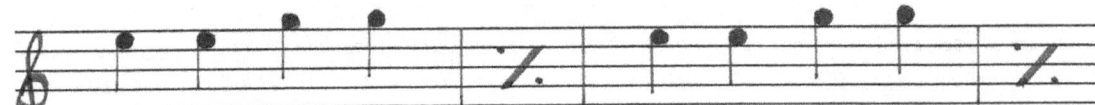

In my lunch-time,   I play hand-ball,

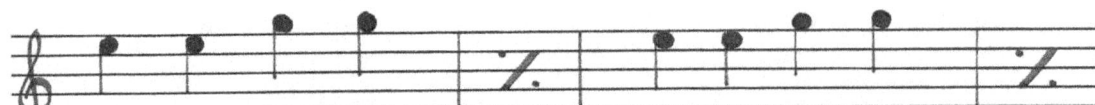

Some of my friends,   we miss roll call.

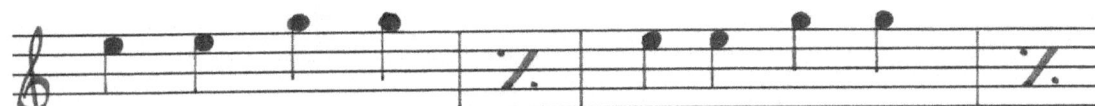

Did-n't eat lunch,   I don't like it,

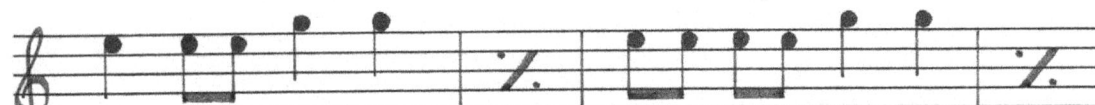

Too much to-mat-o,   I don't like it one bit.

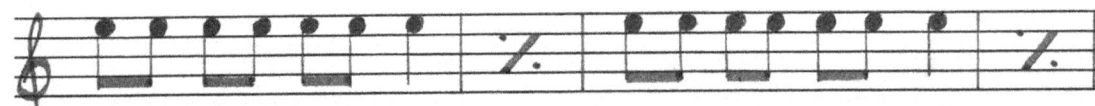

I hate sog-gy sand-wich-es,   I hate sog-gy sand-wich-es.

Some-times my mum,   gives me mo-ney,

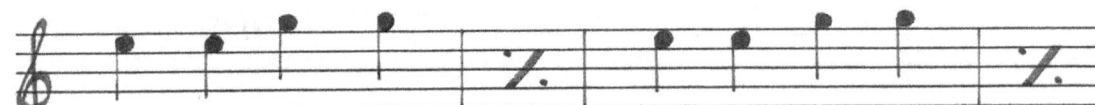

for the tuck-shop,   I get lol-lies.

I hang up-side down,   on the mon-key bars,

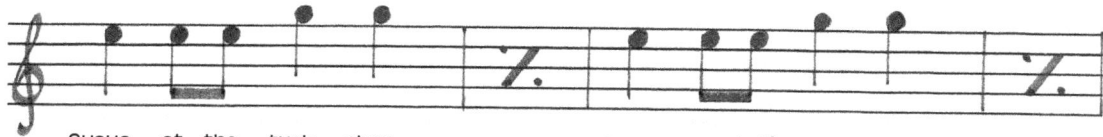

Queue   at   the   tuck – shop,   my   poc – ket's emp - ty.

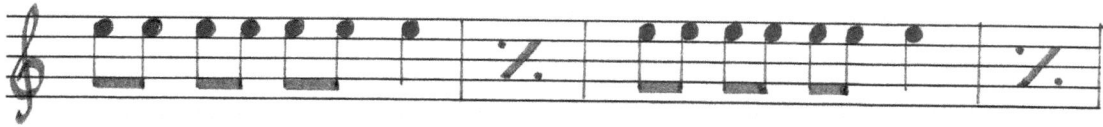

I   hate sog-gy sand-wich - es,   I hate sog-gy sand-wich -es,

tacet

I hate sog-gy sand-wich- es,   I hate   sog-gy sand-wich-es,

I shouldn't talk with my mouth full, but let's get that third finger working! This is a song based around a simple finger exercise and uses two notes.

- Can you tell your teacher what they are?

You know that as music moves up by step, the note names advance alphabetically.

- "Count" up the steps to help you work out the missing notes.

A __ C   C __ E   E __ G   A __ __ D   F __ __ B

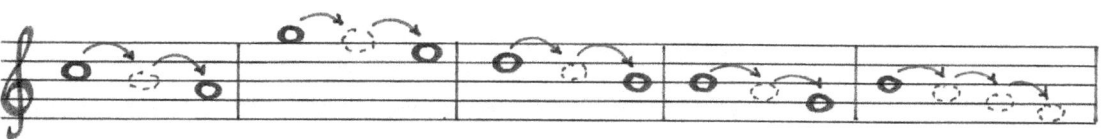

C __ A   G __ E   D __ B   B __ G   B __ __ __

- Count up the steps on the stave to work out the unknown notes.

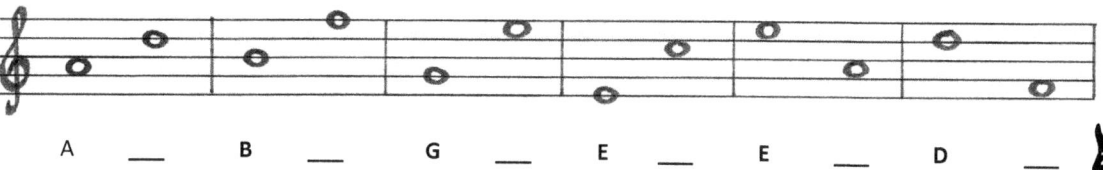

A __   B __   G __   E __   E __   D __

slow blues

Let's really get that third finger moving! Now we're going to move it over two strings. This is a real advancement in your coordination skills!

This note is called "D". It's on the 3rd fret of the 2nd string. Now you know two "D" notes! Will it sound higher or lower than the one you already know?

- Can you show your teacher the D notes in this piece? (ask your teacher to place a new sticky dot on your guitar)
- This rhythm is a bit different groovers. What do you think it is?
- There is a pattern in this song too. The first and the second halves are the same except for one small difference. Can you tell what it is?

- D.S stands for "Dal Segno" which means, go back to the sign. 𝄋 Fine means finish.

22

Cupcakes

This song challenges dexterity in the first and third fingers and starts the idea of counting beats.

Ask your teacher to help you count off the right number of beats before you start your phrase.

tacet

1 2 3 4   1 2 3 4

My mum's cup-cakes,   they are soft and   round.

1   2   3   4   1 2 3 4

Un - cle Den – nis   says, "the best   in   town."

I   can't   wait   to   take   a   bite.

1   2   3   4   1 2 3 4   **fine**

Unc – le Den – nis   says, "they taste just   right".

Cup - cakes,   cup - cakes,   cup - cakes,   cup - cakes,

D.S al fine

Cup - cakes,   cup - cakes,   cupcakes, cupcakes, cupcakes, cupcakes.

23

I L♥VE F⚽⚽TBALL!

Pres-ton plays at   full - back,   Scott, he   plays at   half - back,

Gav - in plays at sec-ond   row,   Na-than, he's my friend you know.

Tit - ans,   Tit - ans,

Tit - ans,   Tit - ans,

x3

I   love   foot - ball,   I   love   foot - ball.

This song introduces the "C" note and the "tie". It also reinforces notes and rhythms learnt previously.

Ask your teacher to place a sticky white dot on the first fret of the 2nd string and mark it, "C". Press down firmly with your first finger.

- Don't be too fussy about the rhythm of the tied notes. Saying the word, "Tit-ans" will be close enough.
- Even though three notes are written, you only play two.

24

"I love football" introduces the phrase, "C,G,F,C". This is the first time you will have played so many different notes so close together.

- Make sure you practise this phrase as you will use it again in another song.
- Look at the first three lines of the song. On what note does the song start? Do the notes go up or down? Would the notes become higher or lower sounding? Would the names of the notes go forwards in alphabetical order or backward?

A DAY AT INDY

tacet

I like watch - ing rac - ing cars,

They go by me oh, so fast.

Mak — ing noise as they go past,

Now I go back home at last.

Rockin' Judge says...

This song introduces the "A" note.
Ask your teacher to put a sticky dot on the second fret of the third string. Press the note down firmly with your second finger.

- Sing and clap the rhythm of the words to the recording after your teacher in the simile bar.
- Name the notes in time with the recording.
- Can you see a pattern in each two bar phrase? Did you notice that from the 1st bar to the 2nd bar in each line that the notes move up by step? Did you notice that we start with an open string and then go to the next highest note? (The note where we have the first sticky dot?)
- Remember that as we go up by step, we follow the alphabetical order. Can you remember the note after G in our "musical" alphabet?

25

SCHOOL TODAY -CHORDS

This song introduces a couple of easy chords.

A chord is what you get when you strum several strings at the same time. What's below is a picture of the first three frets of the guitar. When you place your finger on the "C" note and strum the first three strings, you get a C chord. When you place your finger on the "F" note and strum the first four strings, you get a "G7" chord.

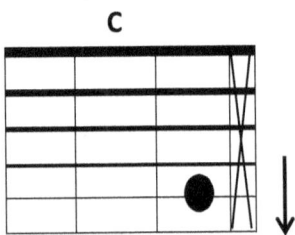

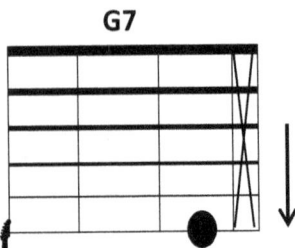

Can you see the thick and thin strings on the guitar diagram? The black dot tells you where to put your first finger and the box with the x through it indicates the "nut" up near the head of the guitar. Hold your finger down firmly and strum "down" in the direction of the arrow. You'll notice the note heads are different in this song. They indicate a chord strum. Strum once for every "ta" and "ta-aa"

Surfing

tacet

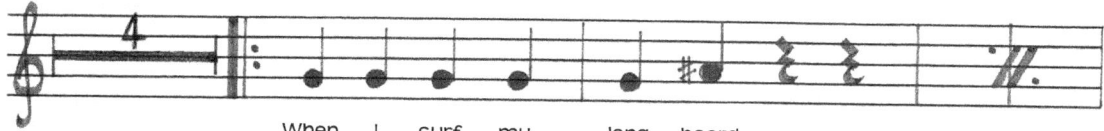

When I surf my long - board,

I get quite a thrill,

Cut back off the wave lip,

Friends watch me from the hill.

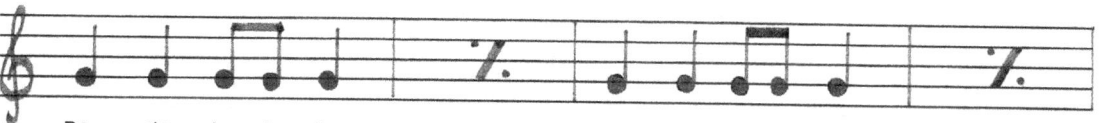

Do, do te te ta, do do te te ta,

When I surf my long - board.

Rockin' Judge says...

This song introduces the sharp. ♯

- When placed in front of a note, the sharp moves that note up in pitch by one fret. So, if "A" is on the 2nd fret, 3rd string, where do you think "A sharp" will be?
- Play "A" and then "A#". Which one sounds higher?
- The sharp will last till the end of the bar.
- Can you find the A sharps in this piece? Tell your teacher where they are.
- Look at the first phrase. Can you find two more phrases that are the same?

This is the worst day, EVER!

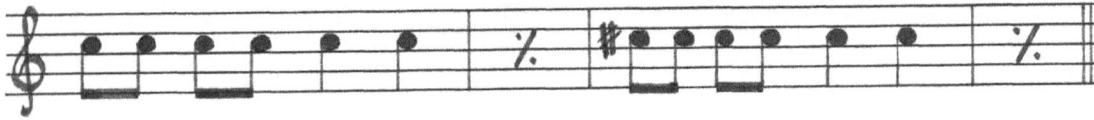

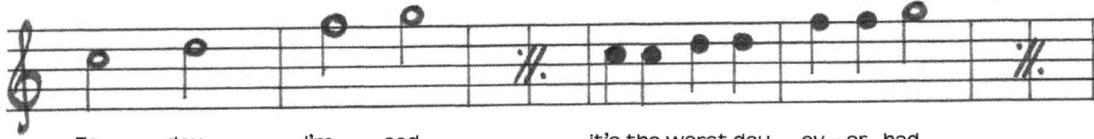

To - day,   I'm   sad,   it's the worst day   ev - er had,

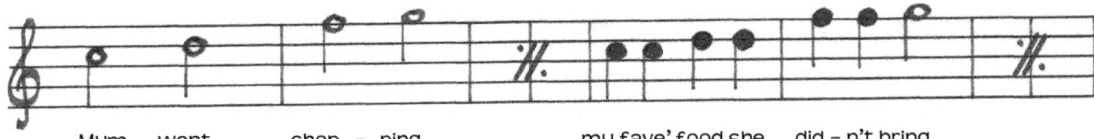

Mum   went   shop - ping,   my fave' food she   did - n't bring.

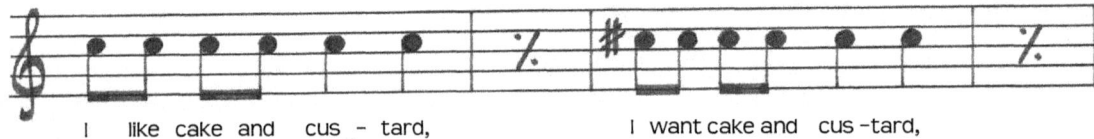

I   like cake and   cus - tard,   I   want cake and   cus -tard,

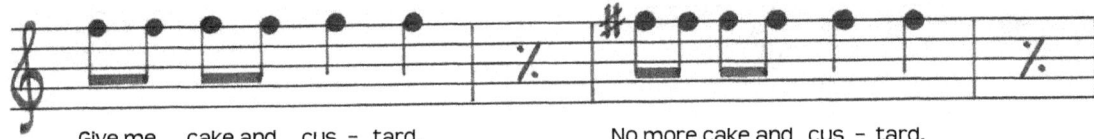

Give me   cake and   cus - tard,   No more cake and   cus - tard.

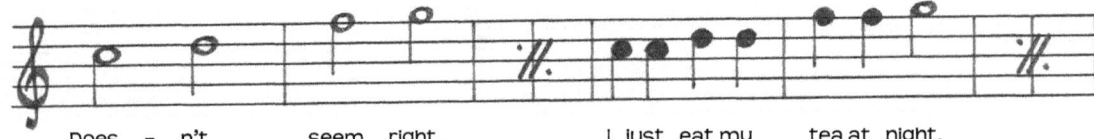

Does - n't   seem   right,   I   just eat my   tea at night,

Hope   the   day   brings,   things to make me   play and sing.

This song aims to improve movement between the first and third fingers.

- In "cupcakes" we used our first and third fingers to move between F and G. Now we're also using them to move between C and D.
- Remember that the sharp is valid till the end of the bar, so if a C# appears, as it does in bar 3, then the rest of the C notes in that bar are also C#.
- This song is built upon two main patterns. Can you find them?
- Look at the rhythm to the words, "I like cake and custard". Where have you seen this?

28

MUM'S VEXATION

tacet

I want this and I want that,

Al - ways take not giv - ing back,

fine

Hard to keep my mind on track.

My time spent is not my own

D.S al fine

I just to - il in my home.

vs 2. I shop for a Fam-il-y, not just you Si-mon you see, please don't have a whinge at me.

vs 3. I like peo-ple who can see, that I work for them, not me, I will love them hap-pil-y.

Have a listen to the introduction to this song. It sounds just like my mum when she's angry!

- This song is based on two patterns. The first pattern is played twice before it shifts to a lower string. The second pattern uses a series of notes going down from E. Can you name them?
- It's easy when notes go up by step but when they go down you have to work out your alphabet backwards!
- Do you remember the prompts that we use to learn the note names on the lines and spaces?

I've got rabbits

tacet

I've got rab - bits, you've got mice,

Stan has cats, that's ver - y nice.

Joe has a dog that's in the yard,

Take him for a walk when he barks too hard.

together

Take him for a walk now, take him for a walk now, take him for a walk now,

fine

Take him for a walk now, I've got rab - bits, I've got rab - bits.

I've got rab - bits, you've got mice,

Stan has cats, that's ver - y nice,

Joe has a dog that's in the yard,

30

Take him for a walk when he barks too hard.

together

Take him for a walk now, take him for a walk now, take him for a walk now,

D.S al fine

Take him for a walk now, I've got rab – bits, I've got rab – bits.

Rockin' Judge says...

This song, as in "Soggy Sandwiches," "Slow Blues" and "Surfing," makes use of an open string to third fret finger movement. However, it commences on the second string, and then later, makes use of the same pattern, but on the first string. The second phrase in this song makes use of another finger pattern, whereby successive fingers on successive frets are used. Here lies the challenge: Drill the second phrase as a finger exercise and then apply it immediately after you have finished repeating your teachers' first phrase. View this as a step toward playing independently!

As you know, a sharp makes a note go up by one fret.

If a C note is on the first fret, a C sharp is on the second fret. If a D is on the third fret, a D sharp is on the fourth fret. If a G is played as an open third string, where will you play G sharp?

Shoe laces

tacet

When we tie our shoe la - ces,

We can go to lots of pla - ces

Won't fall ov - er and get red fa - ces

When we tie our shoe la - ces

NOTE TO TEACHERS.

This song, "Shoe Laces", makes use of a series of ascending phrases. This challenges the student to;

- Name the notes on the score, and will reinforce the knowledge of the relationship that exists between notes ascending by step and the alphabetical order of note names.
- Recognise that as the notes ascend on the score, the pitch of the notes go higher.
- Recognise the alphabetical order of notes on the fingerboard and the relationship to an increase in pitch.

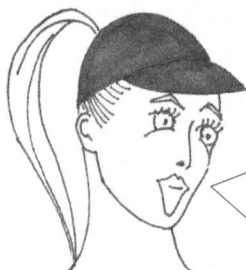

- Hi Guys! Can you see the pattern in the first and second lines?
- You remember how to work out the names of the notes don't you? Every Good Boy Deserves Fruit for the lines and F.A.C.E for the spaces!
- You remember that as notes go up by step, they go up in alphabetical order? What happens in our *musical* alphabet when we get to "G"? What note comes after that? Who said "A" and who said "H"? (A is the correct answer!)
- As the notes advance alphabetically and go higher in pitch and up the stave, you fret the string higher up the neck of the guitar.
- Can you show your teacher which way the higher notes are on the guitar?

Jammin' with the Judge !

My X box

tacet

My X box is num - ber one,

It and I have lots of fun.

Play - ing games with my best chums,

My X box is num - ber one.

Where's my soccer ball?

Have you seen my soc - cer ball?

Where I left it I can't re - call.

I've not seen it here at all,

x3

Where, oh, where's my soc - cer ball?

Hi Guys and Gals. Can you tell me; what note this song starts on? What note this song finishes on? What the name of the lowest note is? What the highest note is? Do the notes move by step or by leap? Can you name the notes as they go up? Can you name the notes as they go down? Which are the high sounding strings? Can you show your teacher which direction on each string you find the high sounding notes? Can you tell me where I might find my soccer ball?

GROMMETS

tacet

Some say I've the mi - das touch,

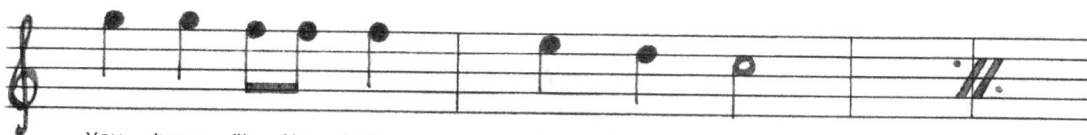

You have lit - tle but I have much.

Be - ing poor is not a fear,

x3

I have gold com-ing from my ears.

- Can you tell your teacher where the notes go up and where they go down?
- Do the notes move by step or by leap?
- What are the note names in the first line?
- What are the note names in the second line?
- What are the note names in the third line?
- Do the notes in the third line look familiar to you? They are the same as..?
- Can you show your teacher the "te tes'"?
- Which notes are faster? Ta or te te?
- The second and the fourth line are almost the same. What is the difference?

My Skateboard

When I ride my skate - board,

Meg - a pipe, it calls me.

How I like to flip and grind,

Ev' - ry one ap - plauds me.

Hi Guys and Gals!

Most of the notes in this song don't move by step but by a
L _ _ _ . You can use the prompts, Every Good Boy
Deserves Fruit and F.A.C.E to help you remember the
names of the notes on the lines and in the spaces. You
could also "count up the steps".

Can you show your teacher which notes are on the lines
and which are in the spaces and name them?

There are two notes that are a step apart. Can you find
them?

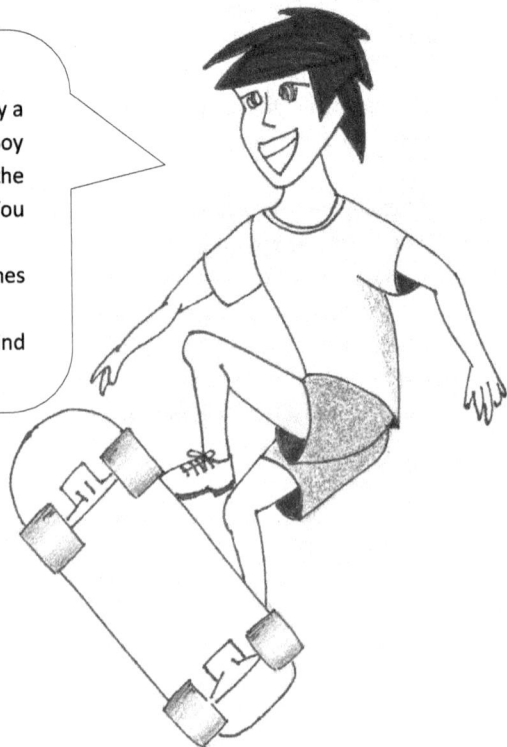

36

My sister eats worms

Hi Guys. This song is a little more complex and may challenge your reading skills!
There are two lines that are almost the same. Can you find them? What is the difference between them?

Yes, Dorothy, that looks quite tricky!
Don't forget to sing the words, clap the rhythm and then name the notes in time with the recording before playing the song on guitar!

tacet

My sis - ter she likes to eat worms.

She just can't get e - nough of those germs.

She will eat them ev' - ry day.

Till my mum says "stop, O - K?"

Breakfast, lunch and dinner

tacet

Eggs on toast for break-fast, ap-ple and sang-as for lunch.

Meat and three veg for din-ner, car-rots and cel-'ry I munch.

I like to be health-y, I like to be strong.

Have a bal-anced di-et, then you can't go wrong.

Rockin' Judge says...

Hi there Groovers, this will get you thinking! Do you remember the chords you played in "School Today-chords"? Remember the G7 and the C chord?

- Can you play the C chord for your teacher? What notes are in the chord that you're strumming?
- Did you say, G,C,E? Can you find G,C,E, written so that you would play all the notes together on the music?
- You can prepare for the C chord by holding down the C note and keeping your finger on it once you've played it so that is still there for the C chord.
- Show your teacher the notes on the lines in the bars on the left hand side. What are their names?
- Show your teacher the notes in the spaces in the bars on the Right hand side. What are their names?

Here's a quick test. Can you remember what these signs mean?

Tacet

MOVING

©Bryce Leader 2011

tacet

Lots of box-es ev'-ry-where, I can't find my fav'-rite pair of

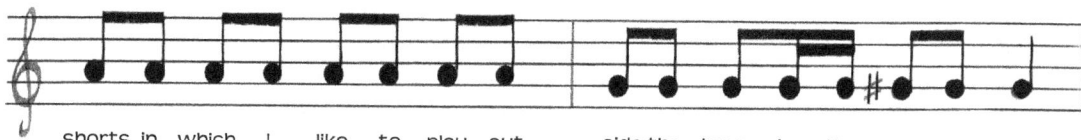

shorts in which I like to play out - side the house in the dirt all day.

Where, oh where have my shorts gone, I'm start-ing to get all for-lorn I

x3

hope I don't need a –noth -er pair, it seems no one ev - en reall - y cares.

Hi there Amigos, This song will really get you playing like a professional! There is no "Copy and Play" in this piece. Your teacher can play with you, but you'll now have to think and play independently!

A note to the teachers. This song is composed of two phrases that make use of a stepwise descending motion that the students have experienced previously. Be sure to drill the students in the note names and the note fingering.

LOST IN SPACE

This song is based on a finger exercise and is designed to improve dexterity between the 1st, 2nd, and 3rd fingers whilst challenging the students to read the notes for themselves.

Note to students.
- Can you find two lines that are almost the same?
- What is the difference?

tacet

Lost in space, my air is low I   can-not find the   way to   go home

To   the   ones that   I   love dear, I   hope I   won't be   wait-ing here too

Long for   res – cue   craft to   come, I'm   hun– gry   and my   time   is   done.

x3

Mo-ther, mo-ther,   mo-ther dear, what's   that you say? Break-fast time is   here?

Bluey, the dog

tacet

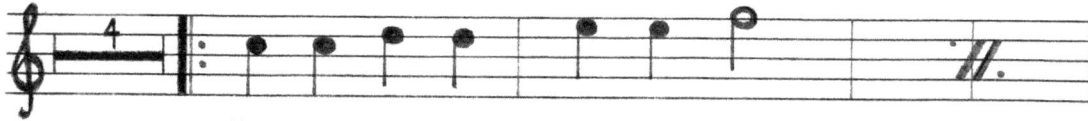

My dog does the great - est tricks,

Bur – ies bones and fa - ces he licks.

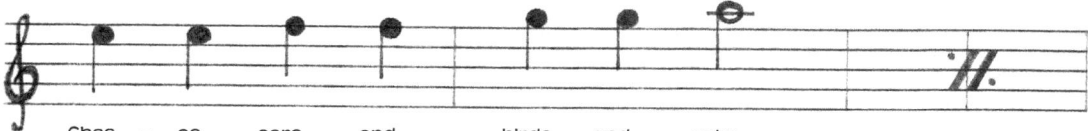

Chas – es cars and birds and cats,

x3

He eats too much and might get fat.

This song introduces the high "A" note.

Ask your teacher to place a sticky dot on the 5th fret of the first string. Play "A" with your fourth finger.

Look at each of the first three lines of music.

- Do the notes go up or down?
- Do the notes move by step or by leap?
- What is the name of the 1st note in each line? Can you work out the others?
- Remember that our *musical* alphabet only goes up to G. What is the name of the note that comes next?
- Can you remember the "C" chord from "Breakfast, Lunch and Dinner"? How many notes did you play all at once?
- Do you remember the "G7" chord from "School Today - chords"? How many strings did you play at once? What are the names of the notes that are in the "G7" chord?
- Can you find a four note chord in this song that use the notes; D,G,B,F?
- Show your teacher how easily you can move from the G7 to the C.

My sister, Dorothy

tacet

Do you want to know some - thing?

My sis - ter, Do - ro - thy, loves to sing,

Go to the park and have a swing,

x3

now you know a - bout ev' - ry thing.

This song is a note reading challenge! Unlike other songs we've played that use a finger pattern or an easy to remember series of notes, this song, "My sister Dorothy", seems to make use of a random series of notes.

Can you tell what song Dorothy is singing?

The sleepover

tacet

Kyle comes to my house, we watch T. V play X box.

To - mor - row we'll ride our bikes put on shoes and socks.

We have break - fast in the morn - ing,

It's still dark though a new day's dawn - ing.

I have a dog his name's "Blue" Kyle's dog's name's "Ro - ver"

Kyle is my best friend we like to have sleep ov - ers.

Te te te te ta ta te te te te ta ta te te te te ta ta te te tete ta ta

Te te te te ta ta te te te te ta ta te te te te ta ta te te tete ta ta.

The "Sleepover" challenge!

You'll notice that there is a third pattern in the last two lines; the notes go up one fret at a time from the note at the start of the line. To develop a professional hand position, make sure your thumb is straight and try keeping your fingers held on to the note once played. By the end of the line, you'll have three fingers on the one string spread across three frets.

The sleepover, part 2!

tacet

My name's Ky - le,   I've a best friend,

His name's, Si - mon,   "Si - mon Wont - Spend"

In their house,   it's so cold,

won't turn the heat - er on,   it' - ll cost them dough.

Their food is "yuk"   their Dad, he snores.

Can't get to sleep,   Help Me, I'm bored!

In the morn - ing,   I've a soc - cer game,

their dog, Blue, is break-ing wind,   think I'll go in - sane.

Rockin' Judge says...

This song introduces two new notes! "E" and "F"!
Ask your teacher to place a sticky dot on the 2nd fret of the fourth string for "E" and one on the 3rd fret of the fourth string for "F". Use your 2nd finger for "E" and your 3rd finger for "F"

There are two patterns in this song. Can you work out the note names and where the notes are located on the guitar? Can you show your teacher the patterns?

E

F

Dorothy's revenge

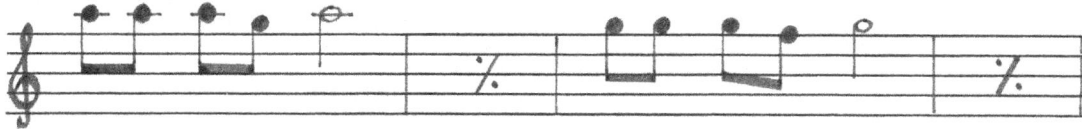

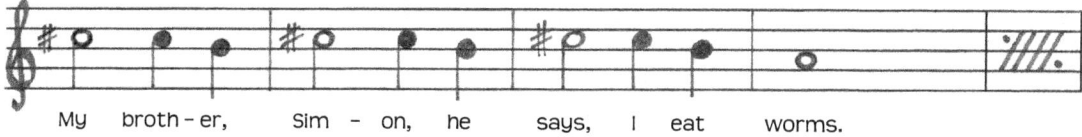

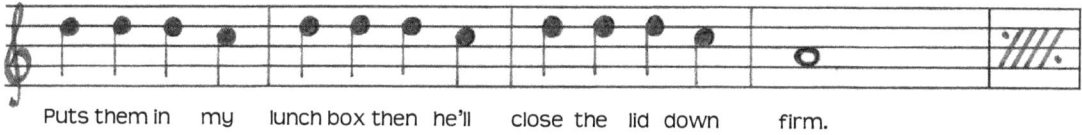

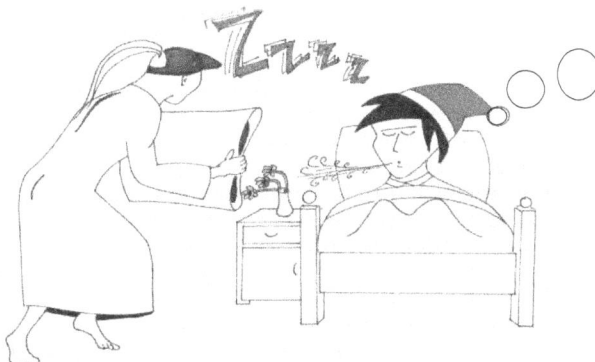

My broth – er, Sim – on, he says, I eat worms.

Puts them in my lunch box then he'll close the lid down firm.

He does – n't know that I know that he snores.

He dreams of space – craft he says, "air is low"

That is be – cause he is try-ing to breathe through my pil – low.

Students, you may now be ready for the quick finger movements and position changes needed to play this piece.

- In the opening bars, prepare your notes by holding the first and third fingers down at the same time. Just lift your third finger to find the note below.

- Can you find the patterns that this piece uses?

Fairyland

1 2 3 4

I've a friend who   says she comes from   fair - y - land.

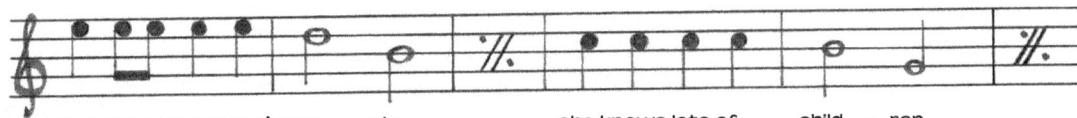

I have a friend who's ma - gic,   she knows lots of   child - ren,

Knows when they all   lose their teeth.   She comes   a - round,

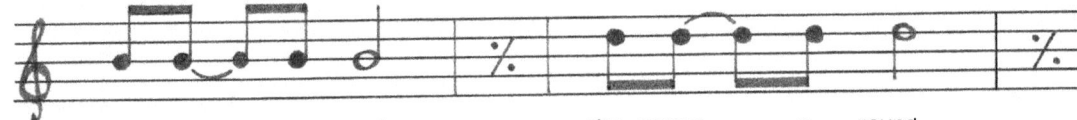

She comes   a - round,   she comes   a - round,

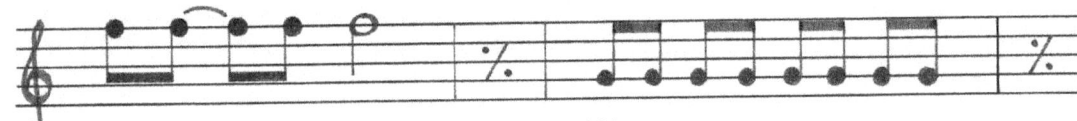

She comes   a - round,   ahhh--------

She comes a-round from   fair - y land,   lots of mon - ey,

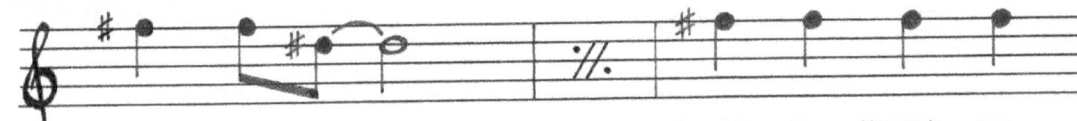

in   her hand.   Sneaks   in   through my

Win - dow,   leaves mon-ey un-der my   pil - low.

1   2   3   4

Fair - y land.

She takes teeth from near and far, turns them all, in – to stars.

Guess you'd bet–ter be a – sleep. She comes a–round, she comes a–round

She comes a–round, she comes a–round, ahhh--------

She comes a – round from fair – y – land, lots of mon–ey

In her hand. Sneaks in through my

Win – dow, leaves mone–y un–der my pil – low

1 2 3 4

Fair – y – land

1 2 3 4

I've a friend who says she comes from fair – y – land

(together)

Fair – y–land, fair – y–land, fair–y – land.

Rockin' Judge says...

Hi there Groovers. Who has ever had a visit from the tooth fairy?

- The opening looks hard, but it uses a fairly simple pattern. Try to work it out before your teacher tells you what it is.
- The body of the song by comparison is quite complex, however, the phrases are short. I'm sure your teacher won't mind you watch their fingers as you learn it.
- Remember the "ties"? They join up two or more notes to make the notes longer. Remember to just play the first one.

Hi Guys. You've been working hard improving the movement between your first and your third fingers, now let's work on our second and fourth fingers. Have a look at the music above the words, "leaves money under my pillow" in the chorus. You might like to "drill" this before you start to play.

What will I do when I grow up?

tacet   **A**

Den-nis, the den-tist, he   pull lots of teeth,

G7

Mich-ael, the but-cher,   he   cut lots of meat.

Em

Hel-en, the ush-er,   will   show you your seat.

C

Kar-rie,   the law-yer,   she   fix lots of grief.

A   G7   Em   C

49

My friend, Kyle

A Sunday BBQ

My dad likes to bar – be – que,

He'll cook you a steak or two.

He can cook it black or blue,

x3

ei – ther way it's hard to chew.

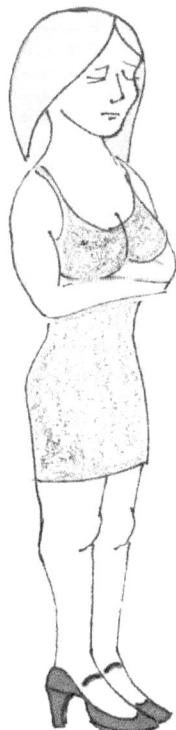

A Sunday BBQ-chords

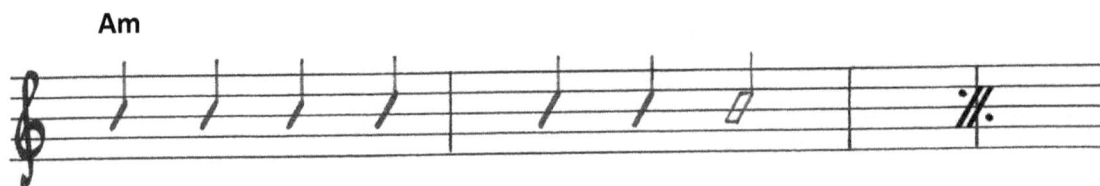

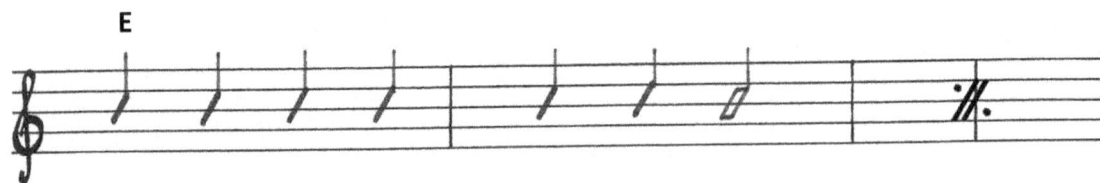

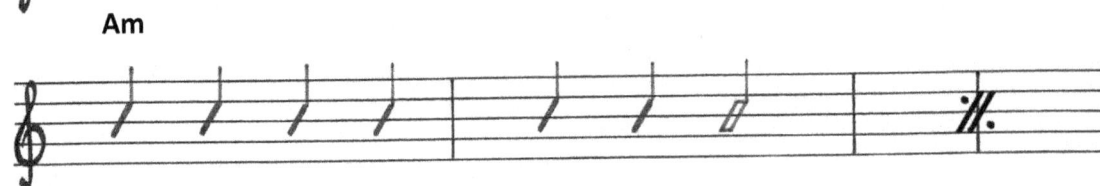

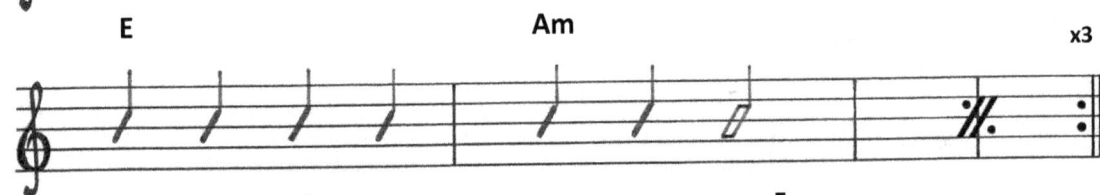

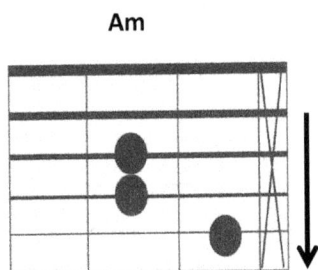

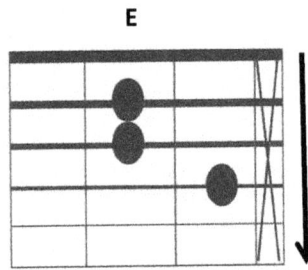

Am

E

Am

E   **Am**   x3

Am   **E**

Rockin' Judge says...

Hi there Groovers! It's time to learn two more chords, Am and E.

- Just as before, strum the number of strings indicated by the arrow and strum once for every "ta" or "ta-aa".
- Look at how similar the "Am" and "E" shape are. You can keep your hand in the same shape and just move it up or down.
- Can you show your teacher which are the low sounding strings on the guitar and which are the low sounding strings on the chord diagram?
- Can you show your teacher the first three frets on the guitar and the first three frets in the diagram?
- Where is the "nut" on the guitar and on the diagram?

NIGEL, THE ATHLETE

My friend, Ni - gel, has a run-ny nose. He take tis - sues

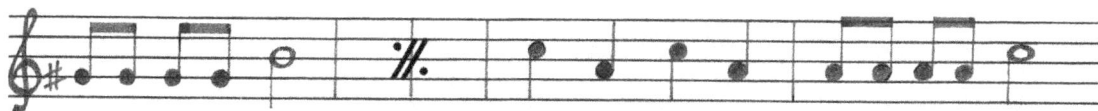

ev' - ry-where he goes. In the school yard, it runs like a hose. *fine*

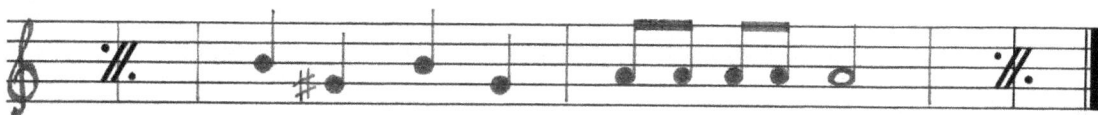

He looks like a wha - le when he blows.

Ni-gel, the ath - lete, his nose likes to run,

he get, his ex-er-cise ly - ing in the sun.

He sneez - es so hard snot goes on ev'-ry - one,

D.C al fine

Ni - gel, the ath - lete has a lot of fun.

Hi Groovers!

- Can you find two phrases that are the same?
- What are the names of the notes in bar 5? (Did you remember that the sharp remains valid till the end of the bar?)
- What do you do at "D.C al fine" and where do you finish?

I'M SIMON'S MOTHER!

tacet

My son, Si - mon,   says his "home-work's too hard"

He is al -ways los – ing things,   lives on   cake and   cus - tard.

Watch - es   foot - ball,   plays   his   X   Box,

Won't wash up   or clean his room,   he has smel - ly shoes and socks.

Please   just   grow   up,   do   as   I   say,

Don't stress your moth-er out,   her hair is turn-ing grey.

I   do   all   the   work,   Si-mon's dad does noth – ing.

He can't ev - en bar – be –que,   it's raw or it's burn – ing.

He is nev-er   at   home,   al-ways at   the cin - e - ma.

54

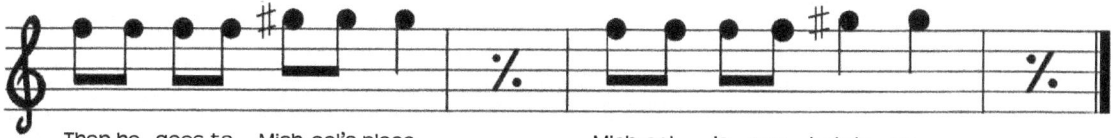

Then he goes to Mich-ael's place.   Mich-ael is our butch-er.

♮ THIS IS CALLED A "NATURAL" SIGN; IT CANCELS THE SHARP. THERE'S ONE USED IN THE SECOND HALF OF THE SONG. CAN YOU FIND IT?

- THIS SONG WILL CERTAINLY TEST THE STRENGTH OF YOUR PINKIE WITH ITS REPETITIVE MOVEMENTS.
- LOOK AT THE FINGER MOVEMENTS IN THE FIRST PHRASE. CAN YOU SEE A SIMILAR MOVEMENT ON THE SECOND STRING?

SIMON

My name's Stan and I've a cat.

My friend, Si - mon, loves a chat.

He'll tell you how rich he is,

He thinks mon - ey drips from his ears.

Of gold, he says he's "got stacks"

He does-n't know it's just ear wax.

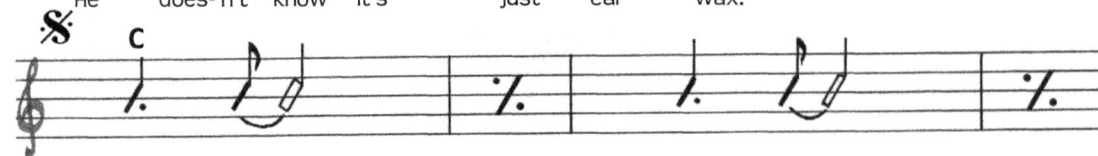

C

Si - mon, Si - mon,

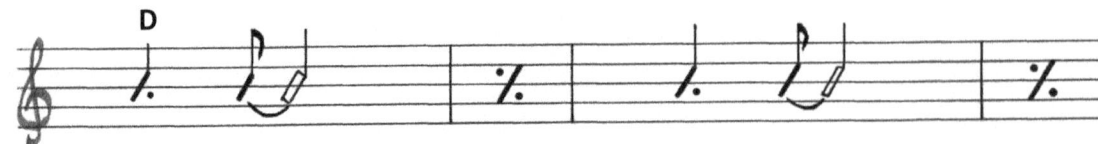

D

Si - mon, Si - mon.

56

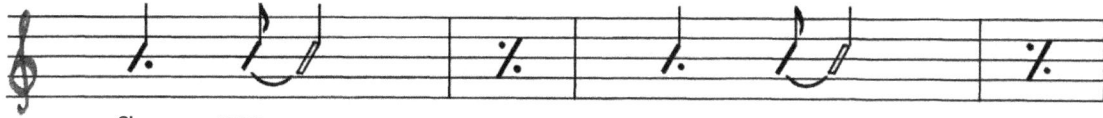

G7

Si - mon.   Si - mon

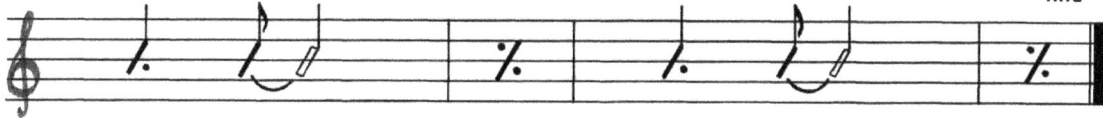

A   fine

Si - mon,   Si - mon.

My friend, Si - mon's   a   good   mate,

would-n't loose his soc-cer ball if   he could   kick it straight.

He   likes   to   ride   his   surf - board,

Thinks he's so   good   we should   all   ap - plaud.

On   and   on   and   on   he'll   rave,   D.S al
fine

He   falls   off   al - most   ev' - ry   wave.

Hi Groovers. I hope you're enjoying making music as much as Simon, Dorothy and I are. You'll notice that this song is made from two themes. The first theme uses a pattern that moves from the first to the second, third, and fourth strings. The second theme uses chords and a rhythm that you're familiar with. Can you remember the name of the song you played that used that rhythm?

NIGEL, THE ATHLETE-CHORDS

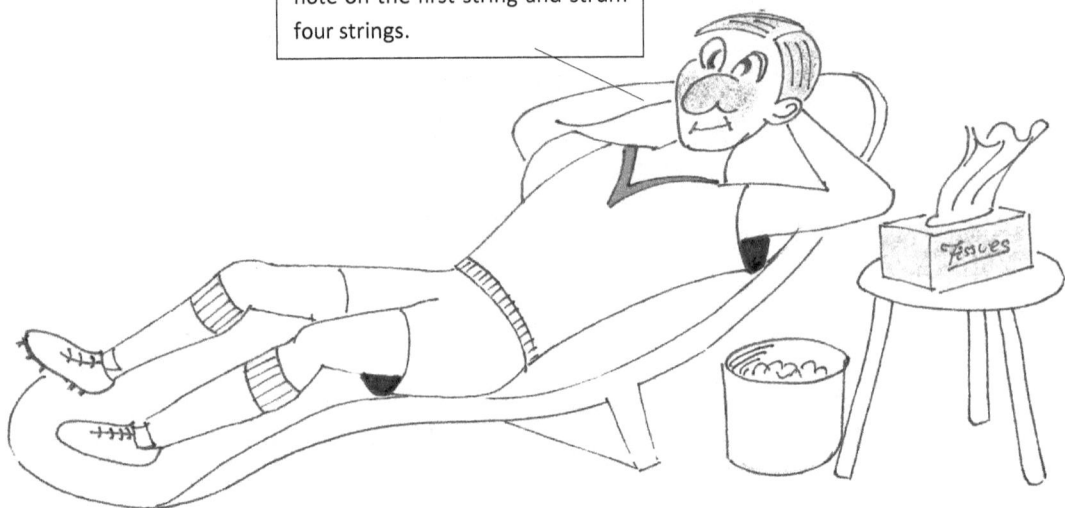

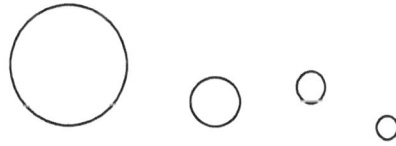

I dreamt Aunty Glennis was the tooth fairy

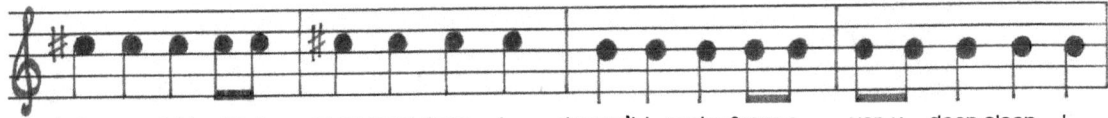

Late one night while I slum-berd deep I dream't I woke from a ver-y deep sleep I

saw Aunty Glennis come through my room wear-ing fair - y wings and mum's per - fume.

"HI" Aunt-y Glenn-is I said quite cheer-y, "you must be mis-tak-en, son, I'm the tooth fair-y" I

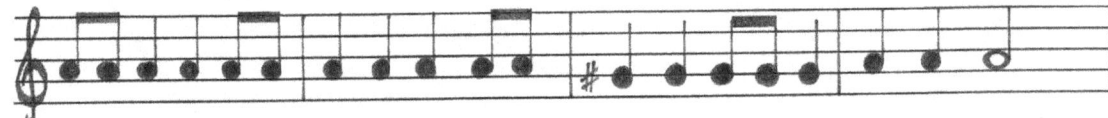

star-ted to cry, she could sense my grief, "but I don't think that I've lost an - y teeth."

I dream't Aunt-y Glenn-is was the tooth fair-y. I dream't Aunt-y Glenn-is was the tooth fair-y

Hey, hey, hey, hey, hey. She

O-pened her hand and what did I see? a lot of teeth and mon-ey for me, I

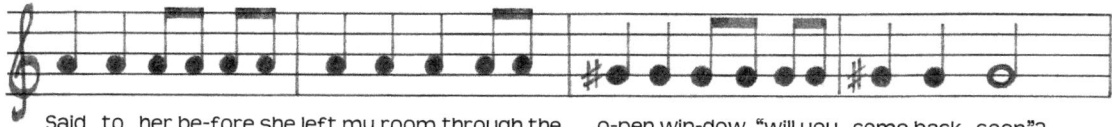

Said to her be-fore she left my room through the o-pen win-dow, "will you come back soon"?

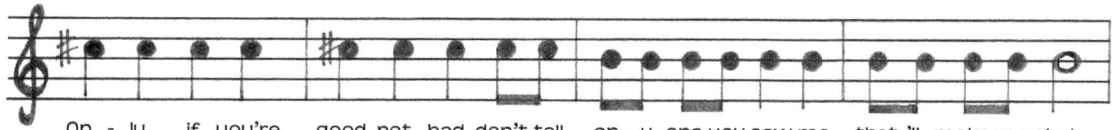

On - ly if you're good not bad, don't tell an - y -one you saw me, that-'ll make me glad.

Now if you'll ex-cuse me, I'll be on my way, please brush your teeth dai-ly and a - void de-cay.

I dream't Aunt-y Glenn-is was the tooth fair - y, I dream't Aunt-y Glenn-is was the tooth fair - y,

She has lots of mon-ey for you and me, I'll keep her lit-tle se-cret but for a fee.

Hey, Hey, Hey, Hey, Hey.

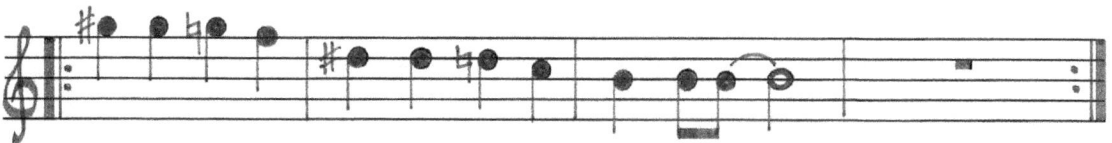

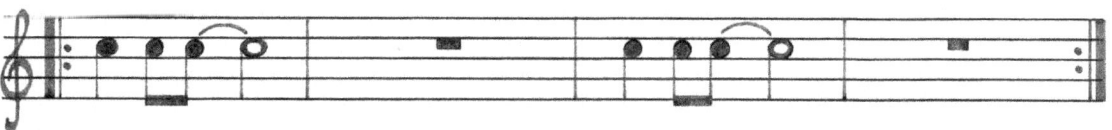

Don't worry guys, it was just a dream. I didn't really blackmail the toothfairy!

Wow! Just like in "Lost in Space" and "Moving", you guys are on your own! Lucky you already know the introduction! Remember playing it in "Fairyland"? You might also recognise that in the verses the notes go down by step and in the chorus' the notes go up by step. Remember too that the sharps remain valid till the end of the bar!

You're angry
because I hate broccoli?

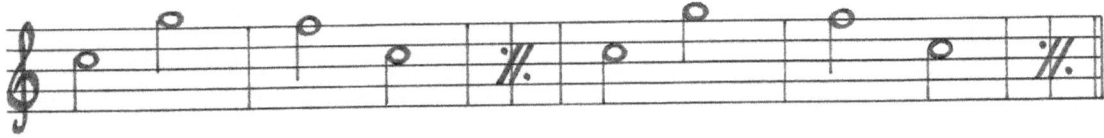

My mum has it in for me, She says I won't eat my tea.

I will eat it hap – pil – y, just don't give me broc – ol – i

I like cake and cus – tard, I like cake and cus – tard,

I like cake and cus – tard, I like cake and cus – tard.

I love foot – ball, I love foot – ball,

I will try to clean my room, wash my dish-es and vac – uum,

try to put my clothes a – way, keep mum hap-py for to – day.

Rockin' Judge says...

Poor Simon, it looks like that broccoli may get a little cold before he gets around to eating it!

- Do you remember playing, "I love football"? Do you remember the chorus? It's the same as our introduction! Show your teacher how well you can play it!

- What about the rhythm to "I like Cake and Custard"? I bet you remember that! Can you show your teacher how it goes? It's only the words and the rhythm that are the same. There is a big stretch between the 1st and the 4th fingers when you have to play the C to the D sharp notes!

Walking the stairs

tacet

Walk-ing up the stairs, walk-ing down the stairs,

a - lone with my thoughts, Blue's gone now who cares?

C

I just want him there. Who will lick my nose?

Em **A**

chew my smel - ly clothes? Chase sticks that I throw?

C

Be there as I grow? Walk - ing up the stairs,

walk-ing down the stairs, a - lone with my thoughts,

Blue's gone now who cares? I just want him there.

I'm a little sad at the moment because Blue has gone missing. Have you had a pet go missing? It's not a nice feeling. I'm sure he'll turn up soon though. He likes playing chasing games. Do you remember what Blue likes to chase?

The lines and spaces that music is written on, the stave or staff, is said to resemble stairs. The high sounding notes are up the top and the low sounding notes down the bottom. They are also in alphabetical order. Make me feel a little better and play me this song. You can do it!

BLUES IN E

©Bryce Leader 2011

Rockin' Judge says...

Hey Groovers, it's been so much fun playing music with you and Simon, and Dorothy and it looks like Simon has his dog back too! Let's finish off this book with a good old "Blues". You know the notes and you know the chords and in the next book that you learn from, you'll probably learn all about counting beats. This tune uses some rests. Your teacher will point them out. (You'll hear the beat but you don't play anything on it.) Here goes, Count me in!

Notes

Lines

Spaces

Name the notes

Name the notes

Name and play the note

Name and play the note

Name and play the note

Name and play the note

Name and play the note

Name and play the note

Name and play the note

Name and play the note

Name and play the note

Name and play the note

Name and play the note

Name and play the note

Name and play the note

Name and play the note

Name and play the notes

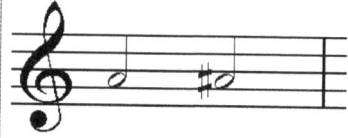

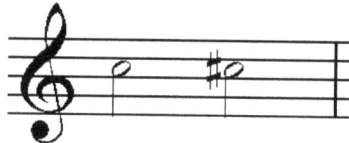

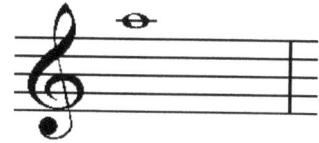

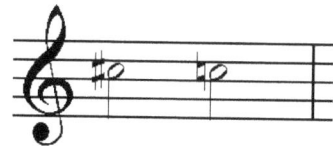

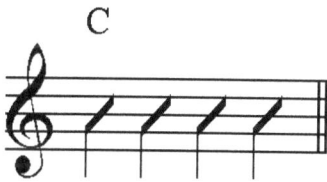

Name and play the notes

Name and play the notes

Name and play the notes

Name and play the notes

Name and play the notes

Name and play the notes

Name and play the notes

Name and play the notes

C

Play the chord

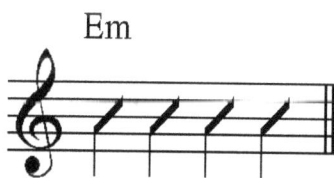

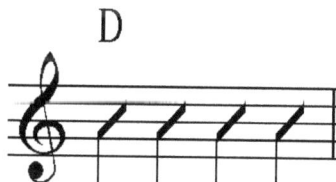

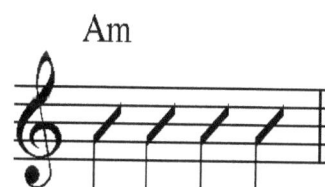

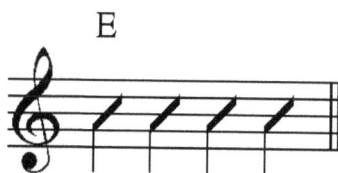

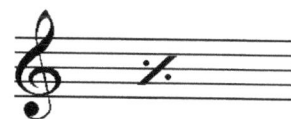

G⁷

Play the chord

A

Play the chord

Em

Play the chord

D

Play the chord

Am

Play the chord

E

Play the chord

G

Play the chord

What does this mean?

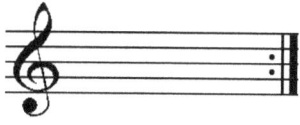

What does this mean?

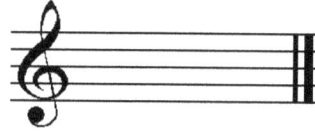

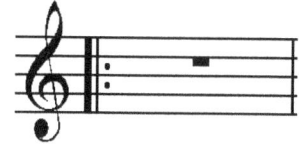

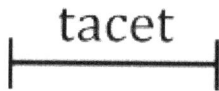

What does this mean?

What does this mean?

tacet

What does this mean?

What is it called? What does it do?

What song is this from? Can you play it?

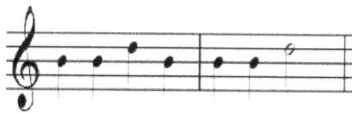

What song is this from? Can you play it?

What song is this from? Can you play it?

What song is this from? Can you play it?

What song is this from? Can you play it?

What song is this from? Can you play it?

What song is this from? Can you play it?

What song is this from? Can you play it?

What song is this from? Can you play it?

What song is this from? Can you play it?

What song is this from? Can you play it?

Name and clap the rhythm

Name and clap the rhythm

Copy, Play & Learn
Guitar

www.ingramcontent.com/pod-product-compliance
Lightning Source LLC
Chambersburg PA
CBHW081300040426

42452CB00014B/2579